FOREWORD

by
His Grace the Duke of Norfolk, Earl Marshal, K

he success of An Outline of Heraldry is v
once again to be able to endorse this fift.

We have one of the oldest hereditary
Queen can trace her descent from the Saxon dynasty of Wessex in the 7th
century. Many families can prove descents from those families who have
made our country great and the records of their pedigrees and coats of arms
are meticulously preserved by the Queen's Heralds, either at the College of
Arms, Queen Victoria Street, London, or, in the case of those of Scottish
descent, in Lyon Office, H.M. New Register House, Edinburgh.

I warmly recommend the reader to visit these offices if his interest is
further stimulated by the colourful pages of this book.

Norfolk.

INTRODUCTION

J.P. Brooke-Little, CVO., MA., FSA
Norroy and Ulster King of Arms

This is a book on heraldry which is different. It is not, as so many heraldry books are, a plagiarism nor is it a
précis of an existing work. It is the author's appreciation of a subject he knows about and loves. The size of
the book at once precludes it from being either definitive or comprehensive, but it does not stop it from being
accurate and I was delighted at the absence of those errors, which writers who are not professional heralds,
and in the nature of things few are, so stolidly repeat generation after generation.

The book consists of a series of brief monographs on some of the more interesting aspects of heraldry.
Some of these will, I hope, appeal to readers and lead them to further study of a subject which really holds
something of interest for almost every civilised and intelligent being. Whether your interest be in logic, art,
design, law, heredity, history, zoology, or bibliography, heraldry can lend it that extra fascination and
colour. Colour – that is what makes heraldry really come alive. Colour is the very essence of heraldry and that
is why this book is so especially attractive; it is full of the most glorious colour.

Finally, I commend this book to the reader because it does not treat heraldry as a dead, historical artefact,
but as the living art and science which it is, especially in Great Britain where we still have royal heralds
designing and granting new arms throughout the Commonwealth. It is cheerful to reflect that for every day
in our modern emaciated working year, the English and Scottish Kings of Arms issue a grant of arms.
Heraldry may be a venerable and noble old lady, but she is very skittish, sometimes to the point of being
downright frivolous.

I have said it before and shall say it again, heraldry is a noble science, an interesting art and makes a
fascinating hobby, but essentially it is fun.

Cover: The Earl of Oxford, Lord Great
Chamberlain, on his charger, and the arms of:
Beaufort; the late Countess of Seafield; Eton
College; Sitwell and Lord Cholmondeley, present
Lord Great Chamberlain.

John Brooke-Little
Norroy and Ulster

Opposite: Arms of King James V from Sir David
Lindsay of the Mount's Register.

1

Seal of William Ferrers, 3rd Earl of Derby

THE ORIGINS AND NATURE OF HERALDRY

Heraldry arose, almost spontaneously, throughout Europe in a short space of time between 1130 – 1160 coinciding with the development of more sophisticated armour. It can be seen from the contemporary seal (above) of William Ferrers, Earl of Derby, that the horseman would be unrecognisable in the encasing helmet, but easily spotted at a distance by the distinctive markings on his shield and on his horses's drapery.

It is generally supposed that heraldic markings were adopted when the face became invisible behind closed helmets, but equally the methods of warfare themselves demanded a system of instant recognition, as faces, after all, can only be discerned at relatively close quarters. Look at the great Bayeux needlework epic of the Norman Conquest. It is almost impossible to distinguish William from Harold – Norman from Saxon. History does not record how many soldiers from both sides clobbered their own companions-in-arms in error.

The signs adopted soon became jealously guarded and objects of pride just as present-day football supporters wear the colours of their teams and so can be instantly recognised and attacked by supporters of opposing teams. A son would inherit his father's markings and carry them in battle with pride. Heraldry, as we know it, had come into being. It flourished especially in the colourful tournaments which were held to give practice in the use of the lance. The armorial decorations at these jousts were supervised by heralds under the aegis of a Marshal and Constable. In these presiding officers we see the origins of the College of Arms.

The social importance of jousting must un-doubtedly have advanced the nature of heraldry to an organised and scientific state. Jousting died out in the 16th century and was revived briefly in 1839 with Lord Eglinton's gorgeous tournament which Scotland's weather put a damper on, but there has been a revival of a milder version of this sport during the last decade at festivals and fairs.

The period when the use of heraldic markings on surcoats and shields served a vital purpose in war was short-lived. The introduction of gunpowder made the sort of armour developed in the 12th century a useless handicap in battle. Heraldry, however, survived independently and flourished. Arms were displayed on seals and this was useful because in the early Middle Ages many of the nobility were illiterate. Arms in stone and on stained glass, silver and elsewhere have provided countless clues for historians in dating and identifying buildings and objects.

As heraldry flourished and became regulated it was necessary to have a language whereby a herald could accurately describe arms and that his descriptions should be comprehensible to other heralds. The language used was Norman French and so it is to this day (see page 13).

Before the rigid regulation of personal coats of arms, they seemed to have been assumed at will and the only records we have of these can be found in the most important of all historic heraldic documents – the rolls of arms. The College of Arms possesses a splendid collection of these rolls including the earliest known one dating from about 1275.

The nature of heraldry, then, is first a system of personal devices appertaining to an individual and continuing, with certain restrictions (as will be seen), for his descendants. It is therefore an hereditary distinction. It is also an art. The proper delineation of coats of arms can achieve a high art form; the animals, objects and charges being highly stylised.

In the 19th century attempts were made to introduce realism into heraldry and this is generally regarded as the nadir of the science. For instance lions as supporters were depicted looking like the sleepy fellows in Regent's Park, and the augmentation granted to Lord Nelson's arms contained a scene on the river Nile complete with palm trees, a disabled ship and a battery in ruins! This is not what heraldry is for. A lion is symbolic and should be made to look the picture of lithe ferocity. A battle should be commemorated by something symbolic such as the Howard augmentation in the arms of the 3rd Duke of Norfolk

Letters Patent issued by the College of Arms under the Earl Marshal's Warrant to the petitioner, Peter Bander van Duren, K.C.S.G., granting him his personal arms, derived from another country, incorporating as a cadency a bordure gules and sable and an augmentation of honour in his crest of the Keys of St. Peter. Similar Letters Patent were issued by the Lord Lyon in Scotland – a unique event in secular heraldry.

and his descendants alluding to Flodden (where the Duke distinguished himself) in which the arms were augmented by a small shield showing the tressured lion of Scotland cut in half with an arrow through its mouth (see inside back cover).

Many purists have also derided the florid shields which appeared in the 18th and 19th centuries as opposed to the plain so-called 'heater' shaped shield of the Middle Ages. However, where arms are displayed in a baroque setting, so long as the rules of heraldry are observed, there would seem to be no objection to them being displayed in baroque or rococo shields if these designs are best for the surroundings. After all heraldry was meant to be decorative.

The actual origins of heraldry are obscure and many writers and historians have speculated on this subject. It is possible that we will never know the precise details but it does not really matter. What *is* important is that this colourful aspect of life arose and continues to brighten men's lives and has provided an endless source of both interest and pride for centuries, and never more so than at the present time.

Left : Compton of Newby Hall. Centre : author's arms with crest of an arm 'vested in Innes tartan' – the key being symbolic of the former hereditary offices of Keeper of Kirkwall Castle and Constable of Orkney. Right : Cavendish of Holker Hall.

Left : Arms of the Duke of Rutland including the famous peacock crest of the Manners family.

Right : Arms of John Churchill, 1st Duke of Marlborough as a Prince of the Holy Roman Empire.

THE PEERAGE – Dukes

A dukedom is the highest non-royal title in the British peerage. Dukes are technically 'princes' and although at first sight it seems that in this country a prince is higher in rank, it must be remembered that Royal children are born princes but are *raised* to the rank of Duke, there being a number of dukedoms used exclusively by royalty – Edinburgh, York, Gloucester, Kent, Sussex and Clarence being examples.

Heraldically a duke is denoted by his coronet which displays strawberry leaves only on a circlet.

The helmet on his arms, as in the case of other peers, faces left and has a closed grill vizor. A duke is addressed as His Grace, a privilege which he shares only with the Archbishops of Canterbury and York. Their younger sons are addressed by prefixing Lord to the Christian and surname and Lady in the case of daughters, i.e. Lord Charles FitzRoy and Lady Henrietta FitzRoy, children of the Duke of Grafton. The eldest sons of dukes have precedence immediately below marquesses and use one of their father's secondary titles by courtesy only. It is often, but not always, a marquessate.

The Duke of Norfolk is Premier Duke of England and is also Earl Marshal. His elder son is known by courtesy as the Earl of Arundel and Surrey, and has precedence below a marquess.

Right : Arms of the Duke of Devonshire, head of the Cavendish family.

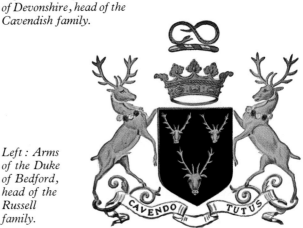

Left : Arms of the Duke of Bedford, head of the Russell family.

Left: Arms of the Marquis of Lothian

Right: The lilies and lions in the arms of the Marquess of Hertford allude to the royal connexions of the Seymours in Tudor times

THE PEERAGE – Marquesses

Arms of the Marquess of Cholmondeley, Lord Great Chamberlain of England

Below: Arms of Robert Cecil, 5th Marquess of Salisbury, K.G.

A marquessate is the second most important title in the peerage. A marquess's coronet alternates strawberry leaves with silver balls.

The premier Marquess of England is the Marquess of Winchester and the present holder of this title lives in Rhodesia. In Scotland the preferred spelling for pre-Union creations is MARQUIS which reflects Scotland's affinity with France. The Marquis of Huntly is Chief of the Clan Gordon and Premier Marquis of Scotland.

The Cecils hold two marquessates, those of Salisbury and Exeter and the last marquessate to be created was that of Willingdon in 1936 conferred upon a former Viceroy of India.

A Marquess is 'The Most Hon.' and his children are addressed in a similar way to the children of dukes, the eldest son bearing one of his father's subsidiary titles by courtesy.

The title derives from 'marche', meaning a boundary; a word which survives in The Marches – that once tempestuous borderland between England and Wales. A man in high command defending a frontier of this nature was known as a Lord March. This eventually became Lord Marquess, but the derivation is clearer in the name given to the wife of a marquess – marchioness.

An early recipient was Robert de Vere, 9th Earl of Oxford who was created Marquess of Dublin for life by Richard II.

WHO IS ENTITLED TO BEAR ARMS?

Some fallacies exploded

Firms who advertise in newspapers claiming to be able to find 'your personal crest' should be treated with caution. If it is a *bona fide* genealogical researcher he will explain that his task is to find if you were legally entitled to petition the College of Arms or the Court of the Lord Lyon to matriculate arms. That is to say to try to establish your descent from someone who was legally entitled to bear arms and to re-register them with appropriate additions to the shield showing your position in the family.

Anyone offering to supply your coat of arms 'over the counter' for a sum of money as if he were selling a pound of rump steak cannot do what he is offering.

A coat of arms is obtained only through the heraldic executive and in only two ways – by applying for a grant or by proving descent from someone who was legally entitled to use arms. Being of the same name as a person who possesses armorial bearings does not raise any presumption whatever of entitlement to these arms or any version thereof.

It must always be remembered that 'family crest' is a very loose term. Arms (and therefore crests) are the personal property of the bearer and are only 'family' inasmuch as each member of the family is entitled to use the arms with an appropriate distinguishing mark and with the consent of the appropriate authority. This rule is much more strictly adhered to in Scotland than in England, but it can be seen that a coat of arms is as much a man's property as his shoes or his motor car, the only difference being that he cannot (in England) dispose of it in any way though he can allow it to be used by others in certain circumstances. The Duke of Norfolk, for example, allows his arms to be used by a well-

known firm of jewellers for display on a 'By appointment' sign – a kind of 'Ducal Warrant'.

If you display someone else's arms and pass them off as your own, you are guilty of a civil wrong, though it is not clear how far an English civil court would redress it. In Scotland the Lord Lyon has wide powers under an Act of Parliament to deal with such cases (see page 18).

In this respect Scotland is in a far stronger position than England since the Court of the Lord Lyon sits regularly to hear cases concerning armorial disputes and claims, whereas the Court of Chivalry in England presided over by the Earl Marshal has sat only once in over 200 years

Standard of Sir Henry de Stafford (c. 1475)

and this was on 21st December 1954 to decide a case brought by the City of Manchester against Manchester Palace of Varieties for displaying the city arms without permission. Lyon, on the other hand, is always involved in such cases and has the power to order the removal of offending arms and even their destruction.

It follows from the foregoing that no two people are entitled to use exactly the same coat of arms. The same indignation and horror at this happening can be imagined if two very grand ladies appeared at Ascot wearing splendidly elaborate but identical hats!

The most celebrated case of identical arms was that of Sir Richard Scrope and Sir Robert Grosvenor. Both appeared at a tournament in 1385 wearing the same arms, a gold bend on a blue shield – *azure a bend or*. There was an almighty row and eventually the case was heard before the Marshal and the Constable and the right to use these arms was eventually confirmed to Scrope. Grosvenor had to get himself a new coat of arms. Today the head of the Scropes, Capt. R. L. Scrope of Danby, Yorkshire, bears *azure a bend or*. The head of the Grosvenors, the Duke of Westminster, has to be content with a golden wheatsheaf instead, but the late 2nd Duke of Westminster had his revenge on the Scropes cen-

An example of debased Victorian design – the arms of Lord Leigh

turies after the dispute. His family called their most famous racehorse 'Bend Or', and this became his own nickname.

While on the subject of 'bends' it is as well to lay another fallacy in heraldry. Bastardy is often denoted by a thin bend or bendlet going in the opposite direction to normal across a shield of arms. Sometimes the bendlet does not reach the sides of the shield and it is then known as a 'baton'. Writers, on the other hand, from Victorian novelists to modern fiction writers will *persist* in calling the sign for illegitimacy a 'bar sinister'. Since an heraldic bar is a horizontal one it can be neither dexter nor sinister.

In any case this is now a rare way of denoting illegitimacy, the more favoured method being the *bordure wavy*.

Unless he happens to be a jazz enthusiast, no self-respecting herald would be seen dead blowing a trumpet, yet so many people who do not understand such things always link heralds with the blowing of trumpets. In medieval times when heralds were also royal messengers they were sometimes ushered into the royal presence by a trumpeter on ceremonial occasions – there the connexion ends, but, evidently, the confusion began.

Another but less well-known howler is the use of the term 'The Royal Standard' when referring to the armorial flag which flies over Buckingham Palace or Windsor Castle when the monarch is at home. It is properly called a banner – a standard being a long narrow flag often forked at one end.

Individuals may display their arms in this way and it is usually an armorial banner which is flown on houses and castles when the owner is at home.

The answer to the question at the head of this chapter is that almost any respectable person of reasonable eminence in the community will be granted arms. This means that whoever can afford the not insubstantial fees involved may apply for a grant of arms and though in theory he can be turned down if found unworthy, this seldom happens as such people do not normally apply for grants.

If the petitioner cannot find an armigerous ancestor in the male line, he must petition for a grant of arms – a brand new coat awarded to him alone and, with certain restrictions, to his descendants. Matriculation, or re-registration, can only be effected if the petitioner can prove either his direct legitimate male descent from a grantee of arms, or from someone whose arms were recorded in the Visitations (compilations of arms in the 16th and 17th centuries by heralds) or officially registered in the College.

Once a coat of arms has been granted, it descends, undifferenced, in the male line in the same way as an ordinary U.K. peerage. Younger sons should re-matriculate the original coat of arms with an appropriate distinguishing symbol. If the family dies out in the male line, the arms can be transmitted through an heiress and are then impaled, or borne on an escutcheon of pretence (a small shield in the centre of the main one) with the arms of the husband of the heiress and quartered by their descendants. Such arms cannot be transmitted through the female line unless the husband of the heiress is also armigerous.

Arms were always meant to display – from the earliest times when they proclaimed identity to the present. Some over-proud people, having recently obtained a grant of brand new arms, splash them everywhere and this can be a bit embarrassing in England. Old families tend to be more discreet – using arms mainly on signet rings, writing paper, silver, family monuments, the door panels of their motors and if they live in a castle or mansion, display the arms on a banner which flies from the flagpole to proclaim that the owner is in residence. This practice was and is widespread in Scotland and has been taken on more in England in recent times. It has not been known for people to have carved armorial stones let into the exterior masonry of their houses.

Right : the arms of Scrope – azure, a bend or – and (above) the golden garb or wheatsheaf of Grosvenor taken from Gwillim's 'Display of Heraldry'. See opposite page

7

Though a barony is the oldest peerage title proper, the word 'earl' has much older origins, being derived from the Anglo-Saxon magnate known as an ealdorman who was more of a local ruler than a legislator. The term itself comes ultimately from the word 'jarl' – a powerful Viking noble, so that the title of earl has very ancient roots.

Although the Duke of Norfolk holds the oldest extant English earldom – that of Arundel (1433), the Earl of Shrewsbury is regarded as the premier Earl, his creation dating from 1442.

The origin of the earldom of Mar, the premier earldom of Scotland is, according to an 18th century lawyer, 'lost in its antiquity'. Certainly there were Mormaers (earls) of Mar in the early 12th century and the present holder is the 31st. This earldom, like a number of other Scottish ones, passes through female lines and is at present held by a woman.

It was long the custom for retiring Prime Ministers to be offered a peerage – usually an earldom. Churchill refused a peerage and Sir Harold Wilson accepted a life barony. For a time it looked as if hereditary peerages had been phased out but Mrs. Thatcher revived the custom and Harold Macmillan accepted the earldom of Stockton. At the time of writing Mr. Heath and Mr. Callaghan remain un-enobled.

Up to the seventeenth century an earl was invested by the Sovereign with a sword which was girded around his waist – hence 'a belted earl', a phrase beloved by Victorian novelists and others which alludes to this long extinct ceremony.

An earl's coronet is heraldically depicted as having five silver balls on stalks alternating with four small gold strawberry leaves. The eldest son of an earl always bears one of his father's secondary titles by courtesy and other sons are 'Hons.'. Daughters are styled in the same way as the daughters of dukes and marquesses i.e. Lady Carolyn Howard is the daughter of the late Earl of Carlisle.

Top : The torteaux or red roundels of the Courtenays, Earls of Devon are quartered with the lion azure of the Redvers family, earlier holders of the title

Middle : Arms of the extinct Earls of Berkeley

Left : Arms of the Earls of Warwick

Left: The arms of the late Earl Mountbatten of Burma K.G., drawn by Archbishop Bruno Heim. The supporters are not shown

Right: Arms of the late and last Earl Manvers. The earldom became extinct in 1955

PIE REPONE TE

THE PEERAGE – Viscounts

Viscounts display nine silver balls on a circlet in an heraldic representation of their coronet. Even if a Viscount has a secondary title of baron, this is not used by his heir and all his children are simply 'Hons'. Some heirs to Scottish Viscounts are known as the Master of Somewhereorother. The premier Viscount of Scotland is Lord Falkland and his son, the Hon. Lucius Cary, is known as 'The Master of Falkland'. Such designations are *not* courtesy titles but ancient and honourable Scottish designations in their own right. The heir of the Earl of Caithness would be known as Lord Berriedale by courtesy, but his more ancient and legally recognised title would be 'The Master of Caithness'.

Viscount Hereford is the premier Viscount in England. The title in recent years has been used to reward distinguished statesmen who deserve more than a mere barony to get them into the Lords, but are not so distinguished as to merit an earldom.

Arundell-Monckton, Viscount Galway

CRUCI DUM · SPIRO FIDO

Curzon of Kedleston, Viscount Scarsdale

LET CURZON HOLDE WHAT CURZON HELDE

9

THE HERALDIC EXECUTIVE

Set in the middle of a jungle of hideous modern building and concrete desolation, the College of Arms stands out as one of the finest remaining seventeenth century buildings in London. It stands close to St. Paul's and like that noble church it was re-built after the Great Fire.

The College received its first charter of incorporation from King Richard III in 1484 and is unique. It has no counterpart either in Scotland or any other European country. Within its walls lies the greatest accumulation of heraldic and genealogical material in the world. Sir Anthony Wagner, former Garter now Clarenceux King of Arms, writes of the College's possessions: 'The collections reflect the long and complicated history of the heralds and the intricacy of heraldic and genealogical studies. For the prosecution of those studies they form a superb unrivalled instrument, but an instrument which it requires years of practice and study to use effectively.'

The public is not permitted to consult these records but those who do, have some claim to the 'years of practice and study' since they are the denizens of the College – Kings of Arms, Heralds and Pursuivants. They have archaic and romantic names redolent of the days of chivalry – Garter, Clarenceux and Norroy and Ulster Kings of Arms; Richmond, Somerset, Windsor, Chester, Lancaster and York Heralds and Rouge Croix, Rouge Dragon, Portcullis and Bluemantle Pursuivants. Presiding over these officers of arms is the Duke of Norfolk in his capacity as Earl Marshal, an office which has been hereditary in his family since 1672. In practice, the everyday running of the College is under the eye of Garter Principal King of Arms.

The heralds are in some ways similar to solicitors. They have their own practices and their own clients. These are built up by a rota system.

Each week at the College there is a different officer-in-waiting whose personal banner hangs from the flagpole in the courtyard. Any caller asking for help is directed to the man on duty and any correspondence not directed to anyone in particular goes to him also and enquirers automatically become his clients.

The heralds deal with all matters concerning heraldry, genealogy, ceremonial, peerage law and succession to titles and with the increase in interest not only at home but also in America and the former colonial territories, there is a great deal of work always on hand. One of the duties of the Kings of Arms is the granting of arms, a power delegated to them by the Sovereign in whose name they act. The petitioner works out with a herald the design of the complete achievement and when approved it is painted on vellum by one of the highly skilled heraldic artists employed by the College together with a reference to the proper style and place of residence of the grantee. The patent is signed and sealed by Garter and the provincial King of Arms in whose province the grantee lives. He and his descendants in the male line who inherit these arms are now armigerous.

Anyone can register a pedigree in the College of Arms provided that every fact in it is authenticated beyond reasonable doubt. This saves

The College of Arms, Queen Victoria Street

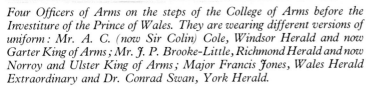

Four Officers of Arms on the steps of the College of Arms before the Investiture of the Prince of Wales. They are wearing different versions of uniform: Mr. A. C. (now Sir Colin) Cole, Windsor Herald and now Garter King of Arms; Mr. J. P. Brooke-Little, Richmond Herald and now Norroy and Ulster King of Arms; Major Francis Jones, Wales Herald Extraordinary and Dr. Conrad Swan, York Herald.

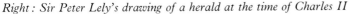

Right: Sir Peter Lely's drawing of a herald at the time of Charles II

a great deal of trouble for one's descendants.

Heralds are present at most important State occasions – the annual Garter Service at Windsor in June, Coronations, Royal and State funerals, the State opening of Parliament etc. Their presence adds an extra splash of colour by their richly emblazoned tabards bearing the royal arms (all officers of the College are Members of the Royal Household).

Sometimes at very important occasions such as a coronation or *honoris causa*, extra officers of arms are appointed and have such names as Arundel Herald Extraordinary or Carnarvon Pursuivant Extraordinary and these are sometimes later absorbed into the College to fill vacancies as they arise.

The Court of the Lord Lyon is very different from the College. Scotland no longer has an Earl Marischal and Lyon is not 'the Scottish equivalent of Garter' as some writers have maintained. For a fuller account of the Scottish heralds see page 18.

Northern Ireland had its own 'Ulster's Office' led by Ulster King of Arms, but the office of Ulster is now combined with Norroy who has been known since 1943 as 'Norroy and Ulster King of Arms'. The Chief Herald of Ireland now presides at the Genealogical Office in Dublin Castle.

The College also possesses an unrivalled collection of Welsh genealogical material and there is an extra-collegiate officer with the designation of Wales Herald Extraordinary.

There have been many very distinguished genealogists who have held the office of Garter King of Arms and lesser posts at the College, but perhaps the most famous of all was Sir John Vanbrugh, Clarenceux King of Arms, the Restoration playwright-turned-architect who designed, *inter alia*, Castle Howard for the 3rd Earl of Carlisle and Blenheim Palace for the 1st Duke of Marlborough. He acted as Garter for three years but was not popular at the College of Arms, partly because he treated their traditions with a certain amount of flippancy but mainly because he was foisted on them by his patron Lord Carlisle, who was Deputy Earl Marshal, and given unfair advancement.

The previous Garter, Sir Anthony Wagner, has written a number of standard works on heraldry, ancestry and the College of Arms itself. He is without doubt the greatest authority on the English aspects of these subjects for very many years.

THE PEERAGE – Barons.

Barons are the lowest rank of peerage, yet baronies are the most ancient of all peerage titles, the premier barony of de Ros being created in 1264, though this being held by a woman, Lord Mowbray, Segrave (created 1283) and Stourton claims to be the premier baron. In an heraldic representation barons display four silver balls on their coronets. Their children are all 'Hons.' and their heirs bear no subsidiary title except, as in many Scottish peerages, where they are entitled to the designation of 'Master'. The eldest son of the premier baron of Scotland, Lord Forbes, is known as 'The Master of Forbes'.

Some of the oldest English baronies, like many Scottish ones, pass through the female line, though most are restricted to heirs male. Life Peers are considered the equals in all respects except that the title dies with them, although their children are 'Hons'.

The arms of Lord Bagot, showing the famous Blithfield goats

Left : Arms of a Baroness in her own right – Lady Braye

Right : The arms of Lord Cobbold, of Knebworth in Hertfordshire

Below : Arms of Lord Barnard

THE BARONETAGE

Queen Victoria considered baronetcies useful for 'ennobling the middle classes' without encumbering them with grand peerages. In this way the Queen underrated the honour.

King James I 'invented' the title in 1611, partly to raise money (dues were involved) and partly to encourage development in the province of Ulster. Baronets were recruited from the old untitled landed families and the minimum requirement for eligibility was the possession of an estate to the value of £1,000. Burke says the first baronets were 'among the best descended gentlemen in the Kingdom'. The present premier baronet of England is Sir Nicholas Bacon, Bt.

The Order of Baronets in Scotland was insti-

Arms of Sir Walter Scott, Bt., matriculated in Lyon Court 12 Jan. 1822. Sir Walter's complete achievement contains supporters as well as crest and motto.

Sitwell, baronet of Renishaw (left) and the arms of the extinct baronetcy of Harpur-Crewe

tuted in 1625 ostensibly to encourage colonisation of Nova Scotia and early patents included grants of land there even though it had fallen to the French. The earliest extant Scottish baronetcy was conferred on Sir Robert Innes, 20th of that Ilk and now held by the Duke of Roxburghe.

Baronets created since the union of Great Britain and Northern Ireland have been 'of the United Kingdom'. All baronets other than those of Nova Scotia bear a small silver shield or canton on their arms charged with 'the bloody hand of Ulster'. Baronets of Nova Scotia suspend the arms of the colony on a ribbon beneath the shield, or display them as an augmentation.

Baronetcies were created widely during the last century and a half to reward distinguished soldiers, politicians, writers (Scott and Hall Caine), Lords Mayor of London, doctors, lawyers, merchant princes and even rich Indian merchants (Jejeebhoy and Jehangir). No baronetcies have been created since December 1964.

THE LANGUAGE OF HERALDRY

Like any other science, heraldry has its own jargon and its own technical terms. Before one can really get to grips with the subject, a basic knowledge is necessary, although in the past too much has often been made of this side of heraldry.

First of all the coat of arms, or 'complete achievement' must be examined. It is perfectly simple. An achievement consists of a shield of arms, usually with the addition of a crest borne upon a helmet (upon which it rests on a wreath) and frequently with a motto beneath. Invariably

Burdett: Azure, two bars or each charged with three martlets gules

Howard: Gules, on a bend indented argent between six crosses botonnée fitchée or, three escallops azure

Hunloke: Azure, a fesse or between three tigers' heads erased of the same, langued gules

Woodruffe: Argent a chevron gules between three crosses pattée fitchée

attached to the helmet is a flowing material known as mantling and deriving from the material used to protect the helmet and the head inside it from extreme heat of the sun. It is now solely decorative and can be used to great artistic effect.

Peers display their coronets between the shield and helmet and peers and others entitled to them have supporters (the human or animal figures either side of the shield – the lion and unicorn in the case of the Royal arms). Allied to the complete achievement are other adjuncts such as badges and insignia. These subjects can be studied at length in standard works on heraldry but they are not within the scope of this booklet.

The crest was borne by a knight in armour on top of his helm as an extra ornament which

The complete achievement of a peer (the Duke of Northumberland) showing crest, mantling, helmet, coronet, supporters, quartered shield of arms and motto

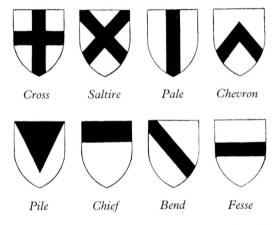

Cross	*Saltire*	*Pale*	*Chevron*
Pile	*Chief*	*Bend*	*Fesse*

became, like the charges on his shield and surcoat, an hereditary symbol. Crests are often used separately from the shield and are always on a wreath or chapeau or issuing from some form of coronet and often with the motto beneath.

Helmets, like coronets, change according to rank. The Sovereign's helmet is gold and barred and faces the beholder. Peers have a silver helmet with gold bars turned in profile to the left. Knights and baronets have an open-vizored steel helmet facing the beholder while esquires and gentlemen have a closed steel helmet facing left. Examples can be seen in the numerous illustrations in this booklet.

Mottoes are not necessarily hereditary and can be adopted and changed at will. In Scotland, and in England where more than one motto has been adopted, they are often displayed above the crest.

It is the actual shield itself which is the most important part of an heraldic achievement. Upon

it are borne the various markings, known as charges, which make up the design. They are used according to ancient conventions and they have strange names. The principal charges are called ordinaries and they are illustrated left. There are hundreds of objects which are used regularly in heraldry but literally anything under the sun and indeed the sun itself (see the arms of Lord Lothian on page 5) may be used in a coat of arms, though of course many things are unsuitable aesthetically.

Badge of the Percys and portcullis badge of Henry VII

The colours on a coat of arms are called tinctures and many have Norman-French names. There are also two metals – silver *(argent)* and gold *(or)*. Red is *gules*, blue is *azure*, green is *vert*, purple is *purpure* and there are others. Furs are also used, the most common being ermine which is depicted by little black tails on white.

One of the cardinal rules of heraldry is that no metal may appear on a metal nor colour upon a colour. Scrope's arms *azure, a bend or* have a metal on a colour. *Argent, a bend or* would not be permissible in heraldry.

When describing or blazoning a coat of arms, rules must be observed. In this way succinct accuracy can be achieved without any possibility of ambiguity and anyone with heraldic knowledge anywhere in the world can understand a description precisely. The field is described first with one word. If it is red, then, simply, *gules*. This is followed by the principal ordinary if any and then lesser charges. Thus if a shield had a red background with a wide band in the middle (a *fesse*) surmounted by a blue five-pointed star (a *mullet*), the correct blazon would be: *gules, on a fesse or, a mullet azure*. Any detailed work on heraldry will give fuller explanations of blazoning, but the best way to understand it is to examine the arms in Burke's or Debrett's Peerages and follow the blazons for them which are given – in this way it will be easily mastered.

Sometimes in printing, where colours cannot be used, a series of lines and dots represent the metals and tinctures. *Argent* is blank, *or* is depicted by dots, *gules* by vertical lines, *azure* by horizontal lines and so on.

Left and right in heraldry become *sinister* and *dexter*, but to make things more difficult, *dexter* is left and *sinister* is right as you are looking at the shield – *dexter* is only right and *sinister* left for the hypothetical person *behind* the shield – a tedious point worth remembering.

Left : arms of Lord Lechmere impaling those of his wife, Lady Elizabeth Howard.

Arms of Lord Lyon Innes of Learney : official arms of Lyon (dexter) impaling personal arms

If an animal has golden claws it is *armed or*. If a lion is standing on its hind legs and looking ahead it is *rampant*, if it is looking out of the shield it is *rampant guardant*, if it is turning right round to look backwards it is *rampant reguardant*. If an animal has a blue tongue it is *langued azure*. If an animal or inanimate object is depicted in its natural colours it is described as *proper*.

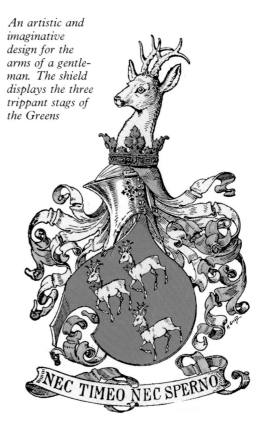

An artistic and imaginative design for the arms of a gentleman. The shield displays the three trippant stags of the Greens

Impaling means dividing the shield down the middle and placing arms in both halves, either the arms of a husband and his wife or a man and his office (see previous column) dexter side (left as you are looking at the shield) and the wife's on the sinister side. *Quartering* is dividing the shield into four or more and having the most important arms (usually the patronymic) in the top left hand quarter and other arms which one is entitled to display through inheritance from heiresses, in the other quarters. Even if the shield is divided into many parts, each part is still called a 'quarter'.

The novice will find it all very intriguing – this strange medieval language, sonorous, dignified yet at the same time slightly unreal. It has the ring of ancient chivalry about it and takes us away, momentarily, from the concrete and exhaust fumes around us. There is also something faintly comical about some of the words. This fact has inspired many heraldic nonsense rhymes, notably by C. W. Scott-Giles Fitzalan Pursuivant Extraordinary. It also prompted Sir Walter Scott to create the character of 'Mum blazon' in his novel *Kenilworth*.

Drury-Lowe of Locko Park

Left: Fownes-Luttrell of Dunster Castle

Right: Wickham-Boynton of Burton Agnes

THE LANDED GENTRY

Writing of the 1920s, James Lees-Milne says 'Even in that decade steel pylons, sagging cables and television aerials were unknown; only the neat, taut telephone wires on wooden poles followed the most important main roads. Ribbon development was just beginning and petrol stations were a rarity. The English landscape was surely the most beautiful in the world, just as the squirearchical system of local government was the best that history had devised for the pre-motor car ages. It was patriarchal, wise and efficient.'

It is true that England never looked better than when it belonged almost exclusively to the landed gentry. It was also, I venture to suggest, a much happier place even though the majority of people were not so materially well off.

Even after two cataclysmic wars and over half a century of punitive and discriminatory taxation and confiscatory land laws which have caused the downfall of countless old landed families and laid their houses into ruins or forced them to be put to baser uses, somehow or other a fraction still carry on. His acreage might be depleted, his

Left: Cartwright formerly of Aynhoe, Northamptonshire

Centre: Bromley-Davenport of Capesthorne Hall, Cheshire. Below: Myddelton of Chirk Castle, Wales

Mundy of Mark-eaton

Left: Washington, formerly of Sulgrave Manor, Northamptonshire

domestics gone and, perhaps, a motorway now rips through his park, but an institution as ancient and as deep rooted as the English squire or the Scottish laird dies hard. Some have survived because of the luck of the game in avoiding Death Duties and some have saved their estates with money gained by an advantageous marriage with an industrial heiress or by going into business themselves and making a go of it. Others have handed their houses, together with a handsome endowment, to the National Trust and remain on as tenants. Now unavoidable Capital Transfer Tax threatens to give the *coup de grace* in the bogus name of 'equality'.

One thing of which no amount of taxation and class legislation can deprive a family is its coat of arms. Among the landed gentry are some of the oldest (and therefore the simplest) and most honourable armorial bearings. We have already met with Scrope's *azure, a bend or*, but the two *lions passant* of Dymoke, the Queen's Champion and Standard Bearer of England, the silver *chevron* of Fulford of Fulford, the golden *bars* of Cameron of Lochiel are other examples of ancient and simple coats.

As a general rule, untitled gentlemen, unlike peers, do not have supporters in their heraldic achievements, though this is not an inflexible rule. Supporters are sometimes specially granted as a mark of esteem by the Sovereign, and in this day and age it might be considered by some to be a greater honour than knighthood. Some Scottish chiefs such as MacLeod of MacLeod, Mackintosh of that Ilk and Colquhoun of Luss have supporters, as do some knights and baronets but it is still a rarity for people who are not peers.

Above right: Roper of Forde Abbey, Dorset

Arms of Somerset de Chair Esq., of St. Osyth's Priory, Essex, charged with a crescent denoting a second son

The arms of notable landed families are sometimes incorporated into the arms of a local borough or city council (see page 22). The supreme example of this is the national flag of the U.S.A. incorporating the stars and stripes. Though there are other opinions about this, it is considered by many authorities that the charges on the Washington coat of arms were used as a basis for the design of the flag. The original arms of Washington of Sulgrave Manor are reproduced above.

SCOTTISH HERALDRY

The early history and development of heraldry in Scotland did not differ much from what was going on in England or indeed any other country in Europe in the mid-twelfth century. To understand the many differences which later developed between the two systems of armory, one has first to look at the national characteristics of the respective races.

Family pride in England has always existed but is usually played down. The subject, except in the cases of occasional flamboyant individuals, has always been subject to a throw-away attitude in

England. It has never been considered quite 'the thing' to talk about one's forbears or to cover one's possessions with crests and coronets. In Europe there have never been any such inhibitions. Great continental families have always been careful not to indulge in the luxury of *mésalliances* and those who have stepped out of line have suffered socially in consequence. A group of German nobles will happily spend an hour or two discussing their respective ancestors and relationships. The French noblesse have always been intensely proud of their ancestry, the Spanish even more so. Scotland, which for centuries had more affinity with European countries and France in particular than it ever had with England, her traditional enemy, has inherited many continental traits, not least that of family pride. Lairds enjoy telling you to whom they are related or from whom they descend – much to

the discomfiture of embarrassed sassenachs. There is not much boasting in this, it is a genuine pleasure and feeling for pedigree and family connexions. The old clan system also has a great deal to do with this attitude – a system where social divisions were vertical rather than horizontal as in England.

Thus heraldry meant that little bit more to the Scot and the result is that he enjoys a much more regulated and logical system of heraldic practice. This is particularly true where cadet families are concerned. The system of differencing in Scotland varies greatly from the elementary labels, crescents and annulets used to denote the precedence of sons in England. In Scotland the Lord Lyon will come down hard on anyone whose arms are not strictly correct and matriculated in Lyon Office. Younger sons and cadet branches *must* consult Lyon before their arms can be properly regularised and used.

There is no equivalent in Scotland of the Earl Marshal nor of the College of Arms. The man in sole charge is the Lord Lyon King of Arms. He

Left: The Great Seal of King David II displays the tressured lion of the Kings of Scots

Seal of Mary Queen of Scots

The Royal Arms as used on Her Majesty's Great Seal for Scotland

is historically a more important figure than Garter since he was formerly a Privy Councillor and therefore entitled even now to the style 'Rt. Hon.' He is a great officer of State and the Sovereign's representative in all matters heraldic and genealogical. What is more, it is treason to strike him! The court of the Lord Lyon is probably the only remaining court of chivalry which is in almost daily use and integrated as part of a national legal system.

Scotland has no ancient rolls of arms as in England and its earliest document of any importance is the *Armorial de Gelré* 1369-1388 preserved in Brussels – a European manuscript with a section on Scottish arms. There are one or two other such continental manuscripts but the first truly Scottish armorial dates only from 1508. The most beautiful record of Scottish arms was compiled by Sir David Lindsay of the Mount, Lord Lyon King of Arms. It is in the National Library of Scotland.

A fuller account of these armorials and indeed of the whole panoply of heraldry in Scotland is to be found in a book called 'Scots Heraldry' by a former Lord Lyon King of Arms, Sir Thomas Innes of Learney, acknowledged as perhaps the greatest authority of all time and a very colourful

and popular personality who did more than anyone else to stimulate and set on a proper course a great renaissance of interest in clan and family history and the great armorial traditions of Scotland. The present Lord Lyon is Malcolm Innes of Edingight, C.V.O., W.S., LL.B., F.S.A.

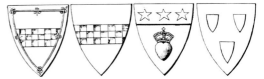

Some historic Scottish coats – Stewart, Lindsay, Douglas and Hay

(Scot.) and Lyon Court, over which he presides, like the College of Arms, has officers of arms – Rothesay, Marchmont and Albany Heralds and Kintyre Carrick and Unicorn Pursuivants. There is also Lyon Clerk and Keeper of the Records. On the other hand these officers are not all in daily attendance in Lyon Court as are their opposite numbers at the College of Arms. They make appearances when required and have ceremonial duties.

The Lord Lyon King of Arms, The Rt. Hon. Malcolm Innes of Edingight with (behind) the late Sir Iain Moncreiffe of that Ilk, Bt., then Albany Herald; Sir Crispin Agnew of Lochnaw, Bt., Unicorn Pursuivant and J.I.D. Pottinger, Islay Herald

19

The Duke of Buccleuch's banner – the Royal Arms of Charles II (with baton sinister denoting illegitimate descent), quartering Campbell of Argyll, Douglas of Drumlanrig and Montagu, Monthermer, Churchill and Brudenell. On an inescutcheon: Scott of Buccleuch

Among his published works are 'Simple Heraldry' (see page 23), 'Simple Customs', 'Blood Royal', 'The Highland Clans' and 'Royal Highness'.

In Scotland only the chiefs and their cadets properly recognised by Lyon can bear the ancient chiefly arms. They are not 'clan arms' and (for example) no man, just because he happens to be called Gordon may bear the arms or any unauthorised version of the arms of the chief of the Gordons, the Marquis of Huntly, unless he can show an undoubted relationship with his chief. In which case appropriate arms will be matriculated for him, otherwise he may apply for a grant of a very different version.

Clansmen, however, may all bear the clan badge without reference to anybody. This is usually the chief's crest surrounded by a strap and buckle bearing a motto.

One of the greatest authorities on all matters heraldic and genealogical in Scotland was the late Sir Iain Moncreiffe of that Ilk, Bt., Ph.D., M.A., LL.B., F.S.A., Albany Herald. An advocate, landowner and Chief of the Moncreiffes, he was an immensely erudite, amusing and eccentric laird whose knowledge of genealogy and heraldry in all their branches was unrivalled.

'Sigillum Domini Roberti Innes de eodem' – a very fine 17th century heraldic seal of Sir Robert Innes of that Ilk – Innes quartering the arms of the Thanes of Aberchirder.

The Duke of Atholl's arms showing quarterings of Atholl, Stewart, Stanley, the Kingdom of Man and an inescutcheon of Murray and the Marquisate of Tullibardine

Unlike England, the succession to armorial bearings may be altered with the help of the due process of the law and they can be transferred between members of the same family in certain circumstances.

Many of the clan chiefs and feudal barons have supporters to their arms whereas in England very few other than peers have this distinction. Lyon has the power to grant supporters to any individual, though their descent is strictly regulated. He can even grant them for life.

Because of the vigorous and strictly regulated practice of heraldry in Scotland and the widespread scattering of Scots all over the globe, Lyon Office is perhaps the most flourishing heraldic executive in the world.

ARMS OF SOME SCOTTISH PEERS

Sir Guy David, 10th Duke of Roxburghe, 11th Baronet and 30th Chief of Clan Innes

Right: the arms of Merlin Sereld Victor Gilbert Hay of Errol, 24th Earl of Errol and 28th Hereditary Lord High Constable of Scotland. He is the son of the late Sir Iain Moncreiffe of that Ilk, Bt., and of the late Countess of Errol.

MacCailean Mor, 12th Duke of Argyll and Chief of the great Clan Campbell

The Earl of Strathmore and Kinghorne – Lyon quartering Bowes (an example of punning or 'canting' heraldry) with an inescutcheon representing the earldom of Kinghorne

Left: Arms of the Hope family as borne by the Marquess of Linlithgow. The crest is an 'impossible' one and not good heraldry

CIVIC, SCHOLASTIC AND ECCLESIASTICAL HERALDRY

A company or a corporation is in many ways treated in law as a person, so that logically, a corporate body is, like an individual, entitled to apply for a grant of arms. Such arms are granted in the same way as personal arms, through the College of Arms or Lyon Court.

Most cities and boroughs throughout the country have their own arms which are displayed on official writing paper, public buildings, the sides of omnibuses and corporation vehicles and many other places. They provide colourful identifying symbols and brighten up and add interest to otherwise mundane, municipal objects. Livery companies, universities, schools, nationalised industries, clubs and indeed any corporate body may apply for arms.

The universities of Oxford and Cambridge have their own arms as universities, but each college has its own separate arms and in those few symbols is enshrined the whole history of these universities so that heraldry can truly justify its oft-quoted description as 'the shorthand of history.'

A number of English towns used arms on their official seals as early as the 14th and 15th centuries, but the earliest known grant was to the town of Gloucester in 1538 followed by Morpeth in 1552. Emblems of kings, saints and castles connected with the places concerned were often used as well as punning arms such as the cow on a bridge for Cowbridge and a church for Eccles. Most civic arms, however, have been granted in the last hundred and fifty years and modern charges such as locomotives appear in some. Often a local family is alluded to in town or county arms. As examples of this the arms of Stamford, Lewes and Halifax all display the blue and gold chequers of the Warren family.

Bishoprics have armorial bearings and these can be impaled with the personal arms of the Bishop. Episcopal arms are often surmounted by a mitre.

Above left: Rugby School. Left: arms of Pluscarden Abbey, Morayshire. Above: arms of Pope John Paul II designed by Archbishop Bruno Heim. Above right: City of Derby. Right: Manchester Corporation.

THE LITERATURE OF HERALDRY AND GENEALOGY

This booklet only claims to give the barest summary of heraldry and it is hoped that those to whom the subject is new will be encouraged to study it further. There is a vast store of heraldic and genealogical literature dating back as far as The Boke of St. Albans, a 15th century treatise on heraldry and hunting, to brand new books on the subject.

One of the earliest classics devoted entirely to heraldry is Gwillim's 'Display of Heraldrie'. The first edition appeared in 1610 and is an interesting thing to own, though later editions were bigger and better. The eighteenth century saw a number of standard works on armory though these are mainly of academic interest only. It is when we come to the 19th and 20th centuries that the great classics of heraldic literature appear. Fox-Davies' 'Complete Guide to Heraldry' is an ambitious work, though it is by no means as complete as it claims. It has recently been re-issued in a magnificent volume annotated by John Brooke-Little, Richmond Herald who has also revised another great classic – Boutell's 'Heraldry'.

Fox-Davies' 'Armorial Families' which came out first in 1929 is also a very ambitious work and the last edition has recently been re-issued in facsimile with many additional coloured plates by the publishing house of David and Charles.

One of the best short introductions is 'Simple Heraldry' by the late Sir Iain Moncreiffe of that Ilk, Albany Herald. It is racily written and amusingly and colourfully illustrated by Don Pottinger, Unicorn Pursuivant.

The books of C. W. Scott-Giles are both readable and instructive – particularly his 'Romance of Heraldry', and Oswald Barron, Horace Round and St. John Hope of an earlier generation have all written learned works on heraldry and genealogy. The most authoritative works of recent years are those by Sir Anthony Wagner (Garter King of Arms 1961-78). His 'Heralds of England' (re-issued 1985) is a massive work of scholarship, but he has written others which do not require a church lectern to read – notably 'Historic Heraldry of Britain', 'Heralds and Heraldry in the Middle Ages', 'English Ancestry' and articles in Chambers' Encyclopaedia under 'Heraldry' and 'Genealogy'.

For Scotland, one cannot do better than read 'Scots Heraldry' by the late Sir Thomas Innes of Learney (revised by his son in a new edition) and the same author's 'Tartans of the Clans and Families of Scotland'.

Genealogy is, of course, closely linked with heraldry and is in some ways inseparable. The genealogy of peers and baronets can be found in Debrett's and Burke's Peerages. The former has appeared more frequently but the latter is easier to consult and contains much more genealogical material. Both volumes are also mines of heraldic information. Copies of Burke's Landed Gentry from 1848 onwards record thousands of families of England, Scotland, Wales and Ireland; their ancestry and their armorial bearings. Two

Arms of the Heraldry Society
granted in 1957

distinguished authorities on these subjects are Mr. Patrick Montague-Smith, former Editor of Debrett and Mr. Peter Townend who was Editor of Burke's Peerage and Landed Gentry from 1960-72. Burke's Extinct Peerages and Extinct Baronetcies are both useful works which have been re-issued in recent times, though they are many years out of date. A more up-to-date work on extinct peerages has been compiled by L. G. Pine. The most exhaustive work of all is 'The Complete Peerage' – a massive compilation in many volumes.

There are very many other works on these subjects but the foregoing are a few important suggestions to be going on with.

The Heraldry Society is the principal private organisation in England which exists for the promotion of interest and research into heraldry. It was founded in 1947 by John Brooke-Little, now Norroy and Ulster King of Arms, and was then called 'The Society of Heraldic Antiquaries'. In 1950 the Society changed its name and came under the control of an elected Council and was

Title-page to the first edition of Gwillim's 'Display of Heraldrie' 1610

incorporated under the Companies Act in 1956 and the following year arms and a badge were granted to the Society. The arms are illustrated on the previous page.

Anyone seriously interested in Heraldry, particularly beginners, could not do better than join the Society which publishes the only national heraldic magazine in Great Britain – the quarterly *Coat of Arms*. The Society, formerly based in Wiltshire, is now at *44-45, Museum Street, WC1A 1LY*.

The Heraldry Society of Scotland publishes an attractive annual called 'The Double Tressure'. The Society is joined by applying to the Membership Secretary, Mr. Stuart Emerson, 25, Craigentinny Crescent, Edinburgh EH7 6QA.

'Heraldry Today' is not only a shop – and an exclusive one at that – but also a publishing house. The shop is the only one left in England dealing exclusively with heraldic and genealogical literature and its attractive premises at 10, Beauchamp Place, Knightsbridge and at Parliament Piece, Ramsbury, near Malborough,

Wiltshire, display a fine collection of English and continental works.

The publishing side of Heraldry Today has produced Rietstap's *Armorial General*, *A European Armorial* and reprints of Burke's *Colonial Gentry*, Marshall's *Genealogists' Guide*, Moule's *Biblitheca Heraldica*, *Royal Heraldry* and the new up-to-date extinct peerage mentioned above.

Another publisher of beautiful heraldic books is Van Duren Publishers Ltd., of Gerards Cross, with *Heraldry in the Catholic Church* by Archbishop Bruno Heim, former Papal Nuncio, and his *Liber Amicorum*. Under the same imprint is Archbishop Cardinale's *Orders of Knighthood Awards and the Holy See* now completely revised by Dr. Bander van Duren. In preparation at the time of writing are: *Heralds of Today, Crests and Mottoes Granted by the Lord Lyon from 1672 to 1982*, and *Heraldry in the Vatican*.

Designed and published by Pilgrim Press Ltd., Lodge Lane, Derby DE1 3HE.

The arms of Braye, Buccleuch, Roxburghe, Northumberland and Innes-Smith were designed and painted by T. Wrigley, ARCA.

The photograph of the Lord Lyon and his heralds is by Robin Gillanders by courtesy of the *Scottish Field*, that of the College of Arms by Newbery Smith Associates. The illustration on page 23 is by courtesy of the Heraldry Society and Mr. C. E. Town. Thanks are due to Dr. Peter Bander van Duren for permission to reproduce the arms of H.H. the Pope and Lord Mountbatten by Archbishop Bruno Heim. The Papal arms are the copyright of the Lyon Archive for Ecclesiastical Heraldry.

Particular thanks for help and advice are due to Mr. John Brooke-Little, Norroy and Ulster King of Arms, the Rt. Hon. Malcolm Innes of Edinght, Lord Lyon King of Arms and to the late Sir Iain Moncreiffe of that Ilk, Bt., Albany Herald, to whose memory this new revised fifth edition is dedicated.

ISBN 0 900594 82 9

© The Pilgrim Press Ltd., Derby. 1986.

Back cover : Arms of some English nobles from a MS in the Bibliotheque de l'Arsenal in Paris reproduced in 'A European Armorial' published by Heraldry Today

Right : Arms of Sir Bernard Burke in his capacity of Ulster King of Arms